# CHILDREN'S BIBLE STORIES

## FROM GENESIS TO DANIEL

# CHILDREN'S BIBLE STORIES

## FROM GENESIS TO DANIEL

RETOLD BY MIRIAM CHAIKIN

PICTURES BY YVONNE GILBERT

**DIAL BOOKS FOR YOUNG READERS**
NEW YORK

Published by Dial Books for Young Readers
A Division of Penguin Books USA Inc.
375 Hudson Street
New York, New York 10014

Created and designed by Halcyon Books, Inc.
Printed in U.S.A.
First Edition

3  5  7  9  10  8  6  4  2

Library of Congress Cataloging in Publication Data

Chaikin, Miriam. Children's Bible stories from Genesis to Danie
retold by Miriam Chaikin; pictures by Yvonne Gilbert.
p.    cm.
Summary: Stories from the Bible, retold
in simple text for younger readers.
ISBN 0-8037-0956-0 (trade).   ISBN 0-8037-0990-0 (library)
1. Bible stories, English [1. Bible stories]
I. Gilbert, Yvonne, ill. II. Title.
BS551.2.C44 1993   221.9'505–dc20   90-42588   CIP   AC

*The art for this book was prepared using colored pencils.
It was then scanner-separated and reproduced
in red, yellow, blue, and black halftones.*

The frontis art depicts the biblical scene in which David
first learns of the challenge made by the giant Goliath
to the Israelites, David's people.

In memory of Peggy Mann
M.C.

For David, who helped me so much
Y.G.

# TABLE OF CONTENTS

n the beginning, before there was a world, there was only God. After some time passed, God decided to make a world, working six days to create one. Each day God made something that was good and useful and also beautiful. There was a sky, with a moon to light the night and a sun to warm the day. And there was the land and the sea, both full of living creatures. Animals walked and leapt and crept on the land and ate the plants that grew there. Fish, large and small, swam in the sea and ate plants that grew there. Birds ate berries that grew on the trees and flew about singing.

God looked at the world and said, "It is good. But something is missing." What was missing was a creature to take care of the earth. The animals couldn't do it for they were wild. A new sort of creature was needed. So God said, "Let us make humans, in my image."

Out of the dust of the earth God made man and woman, Adam and Eve. God breathed life into their nostrils and put them in the Garden of Eden. "Take care of the Garden," God said to them.

God looked at the world again. Nothing was missing. "Now it is very good," God said. Satisfied, God rested the next day, which was the seventh day.

Adam and Eve were happy in the Garden. They had everything without having to work. A river ran

through the Garden, watering the beautiful flowers and many different fruit trees that grew there. Adam and Eve were allowed to eat any fruit they liked. "But not," God said, "the fruit of the Tree of Knowing. Do not even touch it, or you will die."

Adam and Eve didn't mind. They had plenty of other things to eat without the fruit of that tree.

Snake also lived in the Garden. He was smart, crafty, and a troublemaker. He came up to Eve and said, "Did God tell you that you can eat the fruit of every tree in the Garden?"

"No," Eve said. "We can't eat the fruit of the Tree of Knowing. We can't even touch it, or we will die."

"You won't die," Snake said. "Your eyes will be opened, that's all. You will know too much, and be like God."

After that, Eve looked at the tree differently. If she wasn't going to die, why not eat the fruit? Tempted, she took down two pieces, one for herself and one for Adam. As soon as they ate, their eyes were opened. They realized for the first time that they were naked! This knowledge made them ashamed. They quickly covered themselves with fig leaves. And when they heard God coming, they hid.

"Where are you?" God said.

"I hid because I was naked," Adam said.

"Who told you that you were naked?" God said. "Did you eat the fruit of the Tree of Knowing?"

"Eve gave it to me, and I ate it," Adam said.

"Snake made me do it," Eve said.

God was angry and punished them all. "Snake," God said. "I am turning you into the lowest creature on earth. You will crawl on your belly and eat dirt.

"You, Eve, will bear children in pain.

"And you, Adam, you will have to plant your own food, if you want to eat. The work will be very hard. I will make thorns and thistles sprout from the ground. You will have to pull and strain to remove them. Then when you are old, you will die. And you will be buried in the ground. For I made you out of the dust of the earth, and you will become dust again."

As a further punishment, God banished Adam and Eve from the Garden. But was that enough? Would they stay away? They had disobeyed God once; they might do so again and try to return to the Garden.

Now hidden deep in the Garden was another forbidden tree, the Tree of Living Forever. Adam and Eve now had knowledge. If they came back, they would find the Tree, and eat its fruit as well.

God saw to it that this could never happen.

Among the many creatures that God had made were angels. These were winged beings that helped God run the universe. They could turn themselves into any shape. Certain ones, called cherubim, had flaming swords that they spun constantly. They made balls of fire. God put cherubim in the path that led to the Tree, blocking the way there forever.

# Noah and the Flood

Adam and Eve had children, and their children had children. Soon the world was full of people. But the people were not good. They were violent and selfish. They stole and told lies. The sight saddened and disappointed God. "I am sorry I made them," God said. "I will drown the whole world and bring it to an end."

Then God noticed a certain family. A man called Noah, his wife, and their sons and daughters-in-law were good people, kind and gentle. So God decided to drown everyone else, but to let Noah and his family live, and to start a new world with them.

God told Noah to get ready for a great flood. "Build an ark of gopher wood," God said. "Besides your family, take along two beasts of every kind, male and female, and food for everyone."

It was done. The ark was finished. Noah and his family led the animals inside. As soon as they closed the door, the heavens opened and it began to rain. It rained and rained and rained some more. Noah and his family watched from the window. The waters rose even higher. First the earth disappeared from sight, then the mountains. In all the world only the ark floated on top of the water.

Forty days later the rain stopped. The ark came to rest on Ararat, a mountain in Turkey.

"When may we leave the ark?" Noah's wife asked.

"I will send birds to find out for us," Noah said.

He opened the window and sent out a raven. The bird, finding no tree or branch on which to alight, came right back. Noah then sent out a dove. That bird also soon returned. Seven days later he sent the dove out again. To everyone's joy, the bird came back with a newly plucked olive leaf in its beak.

"The water is disappearing," Noah said.

Seven days later he sent the dove out again. The family watched and waited, watched and waited. But the bird did not return.

"That means the earth is dry again," Noah said. "We may leave now."

He opened the door. And everyone – people and animals – left the ark.

Out of gratitude, Noah and his family made a sacrifice to God. They built an altar, lit a fire, and roasted an animal on the flames. That was how ancient people worshiped.

God watched them, these people who would continue the world. Humans are not perfect, God thought. There is an evil corner in their hearts. Perhaps they will learn goodness one day. In the meantime, I made them, and must accept them as they are.

God put a rainbow in the sky. "This is my bow," God said to Noah. "I promise never again to punish the earth for the sins of humans. My bow is a sign of this promise, and will stay among the clouds forever."

# A Tower to Heaven

After the flood, life began all over again. Noah's descendants settled in a country we call Iraq today, near a great river. There, they learned to make bricks by mixing clay and river mud. They made brick houses for themselves and said, "If we can do that, we can do even more." So they built a city. Then they said, "Let us build a tower up to heaven. It will make us famous."

God saw the tower and became very angry. These humans! All the riches of the earth are theirs, but that is not enough. They have to try to reach heaven too.

"I will make a babble of their speech," God said. "I will mix up their language, so they cannot talk to one another."

It was done.

The tower builders looked at each other in surprise. Strange sounds came from their mouths when they spoke. They could not understand one another, and they had to stop working on the tower.

God scattered the people over the face of the earth. They settled various places and formed new nations, each one speaking its own language.

The tower remained unfinished. That city was called Babel, because God made a babble of human speech there.

ncient people believed in many gods. To worship them, they made statues, or idols. They gave them names and called them gods. Then they built fires on an altar, and over the flames they sacrificed animals to the gods. The gods Baal and Astarte had many worshipers. But, as yet, God had none.

Now there was a righteous man named Abraham who lived in the city of Haran, in the north. Abraham did not worship idols. He saw no sense in it. An idol was made of wood or clay. Could a statue make the night and the stars? Or people? Or animals? Or cause food to grow from the ground? Abraham's heart told him that there was only one true God — God who could not be seen, who had made the whole world and all that was in it.

One day God noticed Abraham and said to him, "Leave your country and go to a land that I will show you. I will make you the father of a great nation. I will bless you."

Abraham obeyed God at once. He and his wife Sarah took their servants and all their cattle, silver and gold, and left Haran. When they arrived in a land called Canaan, God said to Abraham, "This is the land I will give to your descendants. You have nothing to fear. I will protect you. Your reward will be great."

Abraham was moved by God's words, but he

wondered about one thing. He and Sarah were both old. They had no children. How could he become the father of a nation?

There was a way, though. In ancient times a wife who couldn't have children gave her husband a second wife as a present. And that is what Sarah did. She gave him her young Egyptian handmaid, Hagar, as a wife. Hagar then had a son, named Ishmael.

Now God wanted to see goodness in the world. And God came to Abraham again and made a pact for goodness with him. God said, "If you walk in my ways and have a pure heart, I will be your God. And you and your people will be my people. And I will bless Sarah and make her a mother of nations and kings."

Honored to be God's first follower, Abraham vowed to walk in God's ways and have a pure heart. But once more he wondered about God's words. How could Sarah become a mother? She was too old to bear children.

One day as he sat outside his tent in the shade of a terebinth tree, he suddenly saw before him three men. That is, they resembled men, but they were really angels. Abraham rose to his feet. "Please rest here in the shade," he said. "I will bring you food and water."

"Do so," they said.

Sarah baked some bread while the servant roasted meat, and Abraham brought the food to the men. Sarah remained inside the tent, hidden in the

shadows, listening to the men speak. She laughed when she heard them say, "In nine months Sarah will have a son."

But nine months later Sarah did have a son. She named him Isaac, which means "laughter."

Now Sara lived in one tent with Isaac, and Hagar lived in another tent with Ishmael. One day Ishmael came to play with Isaac. Sarah grew uneasy as she watched them. Ishmael played roughly with the child. Also, Ishmael was Abraham's firstborn son. By custom a father left his wealth to that son. Was this Abraham's plan? Or would he divide his gold and silver and flocks between his two sons?

Sarah found both ideas unpleasant. She was Abraham's true wife. She had brought him a large dowry when they married. It seemed to her that her son, Isaac, was entitled to all of Abraham's possessions.

So she went to Abraham and said, "Send this slave woman and her son away. I will not have her son be an heir with mine."

Abraham did not wish to send them away. But God said to him, "Do as Sarah says, for through Isaac you will become known. But since Ishmael is also your son, I will make a nation of him."

In the morning Abraham gave Hagar and Ishmael bread and a jug of water, and sent them on their way.

# GOD TESTS ABRAHAM

ow in Canaan where Abraham and Sarah lived, there were many tribes that sacrificed their children to idols. And one day God decided to test Abraham's loyalty. So God said to Abraham, "Take your son, Isaac, whom you love, and sacrifice him on Mount Moriah."

Abraham trusted God, and obeyed. He saddled his donkey and took wood for a fire. And he set out with Isaac and two servants. When they reached the place called Moriah, Abraham said to the servants, "Wait here while the boy and I go up the mountain to worship."

On the way up, Isaac said to Abraham, "Father, I see wood for a fire. But where is the lamb to sacrifice?" "God will provide the lamb, my son," Abraham answered.

Abraham then built an altar and made a fire. But as he raised his knife to slay his son, a voice said, "Do not touch the boy. I see that you love and obey God."

There was a rustling sound, and suddenly a ram appeared in the thicket. It was caught by its horns. "God has provided the sacrifice, my son," Abraham said. He freed the ram and offered it up to God.

Then Abraham went to his people and said, "God hates child sacrifice. You must never do it." And he made it a law.

# Jacob and Esau

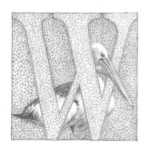

hen Isaac wanted to get married, Abraham and Sarah grew worried. In Canaan where they lived, the people were all idol worshipers. Abraham and Sarah did not want their son to marry a woman who worshiped idols, so they sent him to Haran to visit their relatives. In Haran, Isaac met Rebekah. He married her and brought her back to Canaan.

Rebekah gave birth to twin sons, Esau and Jacob. Esau was born first. Isaac preferred Esau, because he was a skilled hunter. Rebekah preferred Jacob, who had a quiet nature.

In those days the leader of a tribe had great power. He was a chief, a king. Abraham was the first leader of God's tribe. Then Isaac, his son, became the leader. And now, when Isaac was old and blind and thought he was about to die, he called Esau into his tent. "I may die at any moment," Isaac said. "Take your bow and arrow and hunt venison for me. Then cook the stew the way I like it, and bring it in. I will eat, then give you my blessing."

Isaac's words alarmed Rebekah. God heard Isaac. Isaac's blessing would come true. Esau would become the leader of the tribe! Esau, who loved hunting more than anything. Rebekah didn't think he was fit to lead God's tribe. So she called Jacob, *her* favorite, and said, "Bring me two young goats. I will cook them so that they taste like venison. Then you will bring the stew in to your blind father, and get his blessing."

"But Esau is hairy, and I am smooth," Jacob said. "If my father touches me, he will feel the difference."

"I will take care of that," Rebekah said. "Now go."

Jacob returned with the goats, and Rebekah prepared the stew. She took Esau's cloak, which smelled of the outdoors, and put it on Jacob. And she covered Jacob's hands and neck with goatskin, so he would be hairy to the touch. Then, disguised as Esau, Jacob brought the stew in to his father.

"My father," he said as he entered.

"Esau? My firstborn? Is it you?" Isaac asked.

"Yes, Father," Jacob answered. "Here is your stew. Please sit and eat it, then bless me."

"The voice—you sound like Jacob," Isaac said. He took Jacob's hands into his own and felt them. "But the hands are Esau's." Isaac ate his stew. Then he placed his hand on Jacob's head. "May God give you rain for your crops, and corn and wine in abundance," he said. "And may you be great in your own nation, and among other nations as well."

As Jacob left his father, Esau returned. He cooked his stew and brought it in to his father.

"Who is that?" Isaac asked.

"Esau, your firstborn," Esau said.

Isaac knew at once what had happened. The blessing, once given, could not be taken back. "I have been deceived," he said, trembling. "Your brother has taken your blessing."

Esau howled with rage. "Bless me too, Father," he cried. "Please, bless me."

Isaac blessed him, saying, "May God grant you good crops in every season."

When Esau was back in his own tent, he vowed to kill Jacob when Isaac died. A servant came and told Rebekah, so she went in to Isaac and said, "Jacob will marry an idol worshiper if he stays here. Send him to my brother Laban to find a wife."

Isaac sent for Jacob. "I don't want you to marry an idol worshiper," he said. "Go to Laban, in Haran, and take one of his daughters as a wife."

Jacob set out for Haran. When night fell, he put a stone under his head as a pillow and went to sleep. In his dream he saw a ladder. It stretched from earth to heaven, and angels went up and down on it. All night long they went up and down. Then a voice said, "I will give this land to your descendants."

Jacob awoke full of awe. "This place is holy," he said, and he named it Bet-El, which means "house of God."

He arrived in Haran, and there he fell in love with Rachel, Laban's youngest daughter. "I will work for you for seven years, if you will let me marry Rachel," Jacob told Laban. Laban agreed. But he tricked Jacob. After the wedding celebration Jacob went into his tent to wait for Laban to bring in his bride. That was the custom then. Laban did bring in the bride, but it was not Rachel. Rachel had an older sister named Leah. Laban put the bridal veil over Leah's face, and brought her in to Jacob's tent instead.

In the morning Jacob went to Laban and said in anger, "What have you done to me?"

Laban answered, "Leah is older. We do not let a younger sister marry first. Work another seven years, and you may take Rachel too."

Jacob had no choice. He loved Rachel. When seven years passed, he married her too.

Now Leah had many sons, but Rachel was childless. Leah hoped that by giving him sons, and enlarging the tribe, Jacob would come to love her. But he loved only Rachel. Then Rachel too had a son. She called him Joseph.

One day Jacob decided to return to Canaan. He assembled his family and possessions, and left Haran. As he neared his former home, he thought of his brother, Esau. He longed to see Esau and sent a servant to tell Esau so. The servant returned and said, "Esau is on his way to see you. And he has four hundred men with him."

Jacob turned away in alarm. Four hundred men? Was Esau coming to harm him?

For safety's sake, Jacob sent his family to sleep on the other side of the stream. He slept alone. In the night a man came and wrestled with him. Toward dawn the man said, "It is growing light. Let go of me."

Jacob answered, "First, bless me."

The man said, "Hereafter, you will be called Israel. Because you have struggled with God, and with men, and succeeded."

When Jacob woke up and saw his brother in the distance, and saw that Esau was smiling, he was relieved. The two brothers were happy to see each other. They hugged and kissed each other and shed tears of joy. Then Jacob and his family journeyed on.

Now Rachel was pregnant and gave birth on the way. She died, but the baby—a boy—lived. Jacob named his new son Benjamin, which means, "son of the right hand." He buried Rachel in Bet-Lehem and put a stone over the grave. The stone is there to this day.

# Joseph in Egypt

acob had twelve sons, but of them all, he loved Joseph the most. He gave Joseph a beautiful robe as a present. This made the other brothers jealous and they hated Joseph. They hated him for other reasons too. He would tell them his dreams, and in them he was always a king or a ruler.

One day the brothers were out herding their father's sheep. Jacob said to Joseph, "Go see how they are, and come back and tell me."

When the brothers saw Joseph coming, they said, "Let's kill him and put an end to his dreams."

"Our father will never forgive us," one said.

Seeing they were in rocky, thorny wilderness with deep pits in the ground, Reuben said, "Let's just throw him into a pit."

They took off Joseph's beautiful robe and threw him into a pit. Just then, a caravan of spice merchants came by. Instead of leaving Joseph in the pit, the brothers sold him to the merchants—for twenty pieces of silver.

"Come," they said to one another. "Let's smear the robe with lamb's blood. When our father sees it, he will think a wild beast has devoured Joseph." They went back to Jacob and said, "Is this the cloak you gave Joseph?"

Jacob looked at the bloody garment. "A wild beast has taken my son from me!" he cried. "Joseph, beloved son of my beloved wife!" And Jacob wept and grieved for his son.

In Egypt the spice merchants sold Joseph to Potiphar, who was the pharaoh's minister. Joseph was wise, and Potiphar put him in charge of his house. But trouble came one day when Potiphar was away. Potiphar's wife fell in love with Joseph. She went in to Joseph and told him so, but Joseph would not listen to her and sent her away. Insulted and angry, she told her husband that Joseph had tried to kiss her, so Potiphar had Joseph put in prison.

The other prisoners called Joseph "dreamer," because he understood people's dreams. The pharaoh's cupbearer, who was also in prison, told Joseph his dream. Joseph said, "Your dream is telling you that the pharaoh will free you in three days and return you to the palace." And three days later that's just what happened.

The pharaoh himself had a dream. No one in the palace could tell him what it meant. So the cupbearer said, "I met an Israelite in prison who knows the hidden meaning of dreams."

The pharaoh sent for Joseph and said, "In my dream I was standing on the banks of the Nile River. Seven cows appeared, all strong and healthy. Then seven skinny cows came and ate the healthy ones. But they remained as skinny as before."

Joseph replied, "Your dream is telling you this: Egypt will have good crops for seven years. Seven years of poor crops will follow. There will be a famine. But," Joseph added, "you can avoid the famine. Appoint a wise food minister to ration the food."

"I appoint you," said the pharaoh.

When the famine came as Joseph had predicted, Egypt had plenty of food. But the Israelites in neighboring Canaan did not. They were starving. Joseph's father, Jacob, said to his sons, "Why do you sit there looking at one another? Go to Egypt and bring food for us."

All the sons went except Benjamin, the youngest. Benjamin stayed with Jacob because he was the only remaining child of Jacob's beloved Rachel. Jacob was still in mourning for Joseph, Benjamin's only full brother.

In Egypt the brothers came before Joseph to buy food, but so many years had passed that they did not recognize him. He recognized them, though, and he wondered where Benjamin was. To find out, he pretended to be angry. "Who are you?" he said. "Where do you come from? You are spies."

"No, no, lord," they said. "We have come for food. We were twelve brothers. One is no more, and one is with our father."

Joseph longed to see Benjamin. "I will believe you when I see this missing brother of yours," he said. "One of you stay here. The others take food back for your families. But don't return here if the missing brother is not with you."

Simeon stayed in Egypt. The others went back and told Jacob what had happened. "I will not let

33

Benjamin go," Jacob said. "I have lost Joseph. If I lose Benjamin too, I will die."

But the food did not last long. The Israelites were soon hungry again. So Jacob said to his sons, "Go back, then. Bring the man a gift of honey, pistachio nuts, and almonds. And may God move him to release Simeon and return Benjamin to me."

The brothers went back to Egypt. When Joseph saw Benjamin with them, he told his servants to prepare a feast in his house and bring them in. The brothers found Simeon in Joseph's house. They were glad to see him, but they were worried. Why had they been brought to the minister's house? What did he intend to do with them?

When Joseph entered, they bowed to him.

Tears came to Joseph's eyes when he saw Benjamin. He ran from the room to cry alone. Then he returned and sat down with his guests to a fine feast.

The next morning the brothers left. Their sacks were full of grain. But, unknown to them, Benjamin's sack held something more – a silver cup. Joseph had ordered his servant to put it there.

Joseph's guard overtook the brothers on the road and said, "You have taken our master's silver cup!" The brothers were mystified. "We have taken no cup," they said. "Search our sacks." The guards did so, and found the silver cup in Benjamin's sack. The guards led the brothers back to the city, where they threw themselves at Joseph's feet. "We are innocent," they cried.

"The one who took the cup will stay as my slave," Joseph said. "The rest of you, go home to your father."

"Great lord! Equal of the pharaoh," Judah cried. "Please don't do this. Our father still grieves for the first son that he lost. If he loses this son too, he will die."

The words moved Joseph to tears. He ordered all Egyptians to leave the room. Then he turned to his brothers and said, "I am Joseph," and began to cry.

The brothers were speechless.

"Don't blame yourselves," Joseph said. "You see that it was all for the good. God brought me here to save you from starvation. Now go tell my father to come to Egypt and live near me. I will take care of him."

Joseph hugged and kissed Benjamin, and they wept together. Then all the brothers hugged and kissed one another and wept.

# Moses

hen Jacob, Joseph's father, went to Egypt to be near his beloved son, his children and grandchildren and their children went with him. They settled in Goshen, and had more children. Over the next four hundred years their families grew and grew.

A new king came to the throne of Egypt and a new dynasty arose The new pharaoh knew about Joseph and how this Israelite had once saved his country. But now he had only one thought about Israelites—there were too many of them in Egypt.

So he said to his ministers, "Soon there will be more of them than us. Let us enslave them and put them to work in the desert, building new cities for me. The hard work will weaken them and keep them from having more children."

The Israelites slaved in the desert sun, making bricks from straw. Egyptian guards with whips drove them mercilessly. But the pharaoh was disappointed to see that the Israelites continued to have children. So he called in the midwives, the women who helped mothers to give birth. Now in those days sons were more highly prized than daughters. And the pharaoh said to the midwives, "If you see a boy born, kill him. If it is a girl, let her live."

But the midwives did not obey the pharaoh. They killed no children, and boys continued to be born.

So the pharaoh said to the midwives, "Why have you let the boys live?"

They answered, "Israelite infants are born quickly. By the time we arrive, the mother is nursing her child."

More determined than ever, the pharaoh issued a decree to the Egyptian people:

*Throw every Israelite male infant into the Nile River.*

Now Yochebed, an Israelite woman, gave birth to a baby boy. She hid him at home and let no one see him. She had heard that the pharaoh's daughter bathed each morning in the Nile River. So when her son was three months old, Yochebed took a basket, coated it with bitumen and pitch so that it would float, and put the baby inside. And she said to Miriam, her daughter, "Set the basket among the reeds on the banks of the Nile. Then hide in the bulrushes, and see what happens."

Miriam did as she was told. The princess came down to the Nile to bathe. She noticed the basket and told her handmaid to bring it. And when she looked inside and saw a baby boy crying, she said, "It is an Israelite child."

Miriam, hearing the note of pity in the princess's voice, ran forward. "I know an Israelite nursing woman who can suckle the child," she said. "Shall I bring her?"

"Do so," said the princess.

Miriam hurried home and soon returned with her mother.

"Nurse this child for me, and I will pay you," the princess said to Yochebed.

Yochebed took her own baby home and nursed him. And when he was older, she brought him to the palace.

"He'll be my son," the princess said. "Moses means 'I drew him out of water.' That shall be his name."

Moses grew up in the palace. But he knew he was an Israelite. Others knew it as well. One day as he was out walking, he saw an Egyptian guard beating an Israelite. The sight infuriated him. Looking about, seeing no one, he killed the Egyptian and buried him in the sand.

But unknown to Moses, a pair of eyes were watching and he had been seen. The next day he came upon two Israelites fighting, and he asked, "Why do you beat your brother?" One answered, "What will you do? Kill me, as you did the Egyptian?"

Then the matter is known! Moses thought. The pharaoh will learn of it at any moment. Quickly he made plans to leave the city.

When the pharaoh sent his guards to kill Moses, Moses was already on his way out of Egypt.

# Moses Frees the Israelites

oses settled in Midian and married Zipporah, the daughter of Jethro, a local priest. They had a family and lived in their own tent. Jethro had many sheep and goats, and Moses took care of them.

One day as Moses wandered in the wilderness with the sheep, he came to Mount Horeb. (This is another name for Mount Sinai.) He saw a very strange sight. A bush had caught fire. It burned and burned, but still kept its shape. Curious, Moses went up to the bush for a closer look, and a voice called from the flames, "Moses, Moses."

"Here am I," Moses said.

"I am the God of your ancestors," the voice said. "The Israelites in Egypt are miserable. I hear their cries. A different pharaoh now rules. Go to him and tell him you are speaking for me. And say, in my name: 'Let my people go.' Then bring the Israelites here, to worship me."

Moses did not feel up to the task. "Great God," he said, "I stutter, and do not speak well."

Now Moses had a brother named Aaron. And God said, "Take Aaron to speak for you. I will tell you what to say, and you will tell him. The pharaoh will refuse to let the Israelites go. But I will give you wonders and marvels to perform. In the end he will give in."

Moses met his brother Aaron in the desert, and together they journeyed to Egypt. They came before the pharaoh and said, "The God of Israel says, 'Let my people go.'"

The pharaoh laughed. "Who is this God?" he said. Out of spite, he made the Israelites work twice as hard and made their lives more miserable.

Nine times Moses and Aaron asked the pharaoh to let the Israelites go. Each time the pharaoh refused. And every time he did, God sent a plague to punish Egypt. Rivers were turned to blood. Frogs infested Egyptian homes. Lice attacked. Cattle and sheep and camels died. Swarms of flies tormented the Egyptians, and they and their animals were afflicted with boils. Hail and fire poured down on them and locusts covered their food so that they could not eat and darkness settled over their land.

The plagues afflicted only the Egyptians. The Israelites living in Goshen were untouched by them. They were safe.

Each time, the pharaoh asked Moses to end the plague, promising to free the slaves. Every time, Moses did what God told him to do, and the plague came to a halt. But the moment the plague was over, the pharaoh again said no.

So God said to Moses, "I will send one last plague. At midnight the angel of death will slay all firstborn Egyptian sons. Tell the Israelites to smear their doorposts with lamb's blood. The angel will see it and pass over their houses. And tell them to celebrate the passover always. And to eat unleavened bread as a sign that they remember that day."

The Israelites did as they were told. At midnight the angel of death passed over their houses. They were spared. But the night was filled with cries as in one Egyptian house after another, the firstborn son died. The pharaoh's own son also died. Humbled at last, the pharaoh sent for Moses and said, "Go serve your God, and bless me also."

Moses assembled the Israelites and said, "You have seen with your own eyes the marvels God has performed for you. Remember this day always. Teach it to your children. Instruct them to teach it to their children."

After that, Moses led the Israelites out of Egypt. He took them, as God had commanded, toward Mount Sinai to worship God. As they journeyed on, the spirit of God accompanied them, appearing as a pillar of cloud by day and a pillar of flame at night.

# Moses Parts the Waters

he pharaoh brooded about freeing the slaves. "What have I done?" he said to his advisors. Then he sent soldiers in swift chariots to bring the slaves back. The Israelites saw the chariots coming and became alarmed. They turned to Moses in anger and said, "Were there no graves in Egypt, that you brought us here to die?" (They meant, of course, that Moses had delivered them from one danger only to land them in a worse one.)

"Have you already forgotten what God can do?" Moses said.

"You were slaves, and God freed you. You were hungry, and God sent you manna and quails to eat. Now see what else God will do for you."

Moses raised his rod over the sea and a great wind rushed at the waters, separating them in two parts. There was a path between two walls of water and the Israelites crossed safely to the other side.

When the Egyptians started to follow them, Moses raised his rod again. The waters now rushed back to their places, drowning the Egyptians and their horses.

The Israelites celebrated. Moses sang, "God is my strength and song, God is my salvation." Miriam, his sister, led the women in dance, and she sang, "Sing to the greatness of God, who has thrown the horse and his rider into the sea."

# THE TEN COMMANDMENTS

**A**s he had been commanded to do, Moses then brought the Israelites to Sinai, where they were to meet God. They washed and cleansed themselves and assembled at the mountain. And Moses went up the mountain to receive God's laws in writing:

> "I, your God, brought you out of Egypt.
> Worship only me, and me alone.
> Do not use my name falsely.
> Remember the Sabbath day,
> to keep it holy.
> Honor your father and mother.
> Do not murder.
> Do not commit adultery.
> Do not steal.
> Speak the truth.
> Do not desire what belongs to
> your neighbor."

Moses remained on the mountain for many days, and the Israelites began to whisper among themselves, "Where is he?" Then they went to Aaron and said, "Make us an idol, a god to worship. Moses seems to have disappeared." Aaron finally gave in to them. He melted their gold rings and bracelets and made a golden idol in the shape of a calf to worship.

Forty days later, though, Moses came down from

the mountain. In his hands were two clay tablets inscribed with the Ten Commandments. Joshua, his helper, was waiting for him. As they walked to the Israelite camp, they heard strange noises. "Is it the sound of war?" Joshua asked.

"No, it is singing," Moses said.

When Moses arrived at the camp, he found the Israelites singing and dancing around the fire, worshiping a golden calf. Anger boiled up in him, and he threw down the tablets and broke them. "You have sinned a great sin," he cried, and tossed the calf into the flames.

Then he said to Aaron, "What did you do?"

Aaron said, "My lord, do not be angry with me. You know these people. They wanted something to worship. They insisted...."

Moses went back up the mountain for a second copy of the laws. His face was bathed in heavenly light when he came down. And he stood speaking to the Israelites, telling them what God had said.

"We will obey," the people said. And God wanted them to build a tabernacle, a house where they would go to worship God.

The Israelites threw themselves into the task at once. Smiths melted gold and made rods, weavers wove curtains, artists embroidered the curtains with silver and gold. The work was finally finished. And when the building stood, the Israelites saw the glory of God fill the tabernacle.

# Balaam and His Donkey

he Israelites had been slaves for a long time. They didn't know what it meant to be free. So Moses kept them in the wilderness for forty years as he taught them how to have understanding hearts, to be fair, and how to mix justice with mercy. Joshua taught them to fight when they were attacked by hostile tribes.

The Israelites wandered from place to place with their animals. When they came to Moab, they stopped outside the city and put up their tents. Balak, the king of Moab, watched them and became alarmed. He had never seen so many tents.

Now in those days people believed in the power of curses. So the king sent messengers to Balaam, a man who was known for his curses. Speaking for the king, the messengers said, "The people from Egypt are so numerous that their tents cover the earth. Come and curse them for me and I will make you rich."

Balaam answered, "Let me ask God. I can do only what God tells me to do."

God told Balaam not to go. When the king heard this, he sent princes to Balaam and had them offer greater riches still.

Balaam said, "No amount of silver and gold could make me do it. God does not want me to. Let me ask God."

God said to Balaam, "Go with them, but say only

what I tell you to say."

Balaam saddled his donkey and left with them. He must have said something that he shouldn't have, because God sent down an angel with a sword. The angel was invisible to Balaam, but not to the donkey. When the angel appeared on the road, the donkey stepped out of his way.

Balaam beat her with his staff for leaving the road.

The donkey then entered a narrow alley between two walls. She saw the angel and pressed herself against the wall to let him pass. As she did, she squeezed Balaam's foot against the wall. He beat her again. "If this staff were a sword, I'd kill you," he said.

The donkey turned to Balaam and said, "Haven't I served you well all these years? Why do you beat me?"

God opened Balaam's eyes and he saw the angel. "Why did you beat the donkey?" the angel said. "She saved your life. If she had not stepped aside, I would have slain you."

Balaam bowed his head in shame. "I have sinned," he said. "Should I turn back?"

"No," said the angel. "Go on. But say only what God tells you to say. No more, and no less."

The king greeted Balaam at the city gate.

"I have come," Balaam said. "But remember: I cannot bless or curse as I wish. I can do only what God tells me."

The king's priests prepared the mountain for the cursing ceremony. They put up seven altars and

sacrificed a bull and a ram on each. As the smoke rose, the king led Balaam to the place on the mount with the best view. A curse-maker had to look at what he was cursing, or the curse would not work.

Balaam gazed down at the Israelite camp. The tents standing side by side, looked pleasant and orderly. The sight filled him with peace, and he said,

> "How goodly are your tents, O Israel!
> Like gardens along the river,
> Like aloes planted by God.
> Blessed be those who bless you,
> And cursed be those who curse you."

"What?" the king said in anger. "I bring you here to curse the Israelites, and you bless them!"

"I told you," Balaam said. "I can say only what God tells me to say. No more, and no less."

So Balaam went down from the mount and returned home with his donkey.

# Deborah's Victory Song

 oses died on the plains of Moab. The Israelites buried him in an unmarked place so that people would not go there to worship him instead of God.

Then the Israelites invaded Canaan. And as God had commanded, they drove out the idol worshipers and smashed their idols and altars. And they set up their tabernacle to God and became one nation.

But they did not drive out all the idol worshipers. Some were still there. And some Israelites began to worship idols.

God saw them and sent down an angel to say: "I kept my promise to you. I gave you this land. But you have not kept your promise to worship only me."

The Israelites were ashamed and began to cry. And they began to worship only God again.

They called the place Bochim, or "the criers."

But the Israelites soon forgot God again. They began to worship idols once more, until they were conquered by King Jabin and his general, Sisera. Again they cried out to God for help.

Deborah was wise and holy. One day as she sat under her palm tree, God told her how to defeat Sisera. So she sent for Barak, the Israelite captain, and said, "Go to the top of Mount Tabor to fight Sisera."

Barak said, "I will go if you come with me."

And Deborah said, "If I go with you, people will say the victory was mine, not yours."

They set out together: Deborah, Barak, and the Israelite fighters. Another tribe, the Kenites, were friends of theirs, and the Israelites refreshed themselves at the Kenite camp, then went on. But the Kenites were friends of Sisera as well, and they told him that the Israelites were on Mount Tabor. Sisera gathered his warriors and went to make war.

"He has come," Deborah said to Barak. "Go down and fight."

Barak and his men went down and smote Sisera's fighters with their swords. Sisera himself escaped. When Barak saw that Sisera was not among the fallen, he went looking for him.

Sisera was in the Kenite camp, hiding in the tent of Jael, a Kenite woman. She covered him with a blanket and gave him milk to drink. When he fell asleep, she drove a tent pin through his temple. Then she went out to find Barak. "Come inside," she said to him. "You will see the one you are looking for." Barak followed her into the tent and saw Sisera lying dead.

The Israelites rejoiced. Deborah sang a victory song.

> *"Those who joined us willingly,*
> *My heart goes out to you.*
> *You who ride on white donkeys,*
> *You who sit on silks and satins,*
> *You who are passing through,*
> *Tell everyone about our victory.*
> *And bless the name of Jael."*

Deborah felt sorry for Sisera's mother and added,

*"Through the window she looks,*
*Wondering why his chariot has not come.*
*Her princesses console her,*
*They say he is dividing the spoils,*
*Giving his men two damsels each,*
*And embroidered garments to wear.*
*So they tell her,*
*But Sisera will not come."*

# Samson and Delilah

eople known as Philistines came to Canaan and settled on the coast. They began to attack the Israelites. At that time the Israelites had no leader, no one to fight for them, and they were defenseless. Then an angel came to an Israelite woman and said, "You will have a son who will begin to save Israel. Never cut his hair, for that will be the secret of his strength."

The woman gave birth to a son whom she called Samson. He was simple, but big and strong. When he was grown, he went to ask a Philistine woman he liked to marry him. On the way he met a lion. With his bare hands he tore the beast apart.

When the woman agreed to marry him, Samson went home to tell his mother and father. As he went past the lion, he noticed bees swarming around it. He went to look. The carcass was full of honey, and he reached in and scraped out a supply. Some he ate on the way. The rest he brought home to his parents.

They were not pleased to hear that he wanted to marry a Philistine woman, but they went to meet her family anyway. Samson made a wedding feast and invited thirty Philistine men. He gave them food and drink and entertained them with riddles. "Answer this one in seven days, and I will give each of you a shirt and a robe," he said. "If you can't, you give me sixty garments."

"Tell us your riddle," the Philistines said.
Samson said:

> "Out of the eater came food,
>   And out of the strong came sweetness."

The Philistines could not find the right answer. At the end of the sixth day they went to Samson's bride. "Find the answer for us," they said, "or we will burn down your father's house, with you in it. We did not come here to become paupers."

Samson's bride said to him, "What is the answer? You can tell me. I'm your wife."

Samson said, "I haven't told even my parents. But I will tell you." And he told her about finding honey in the carcass of a lion. She told the Philistines, and they said to Samson,

> "A living lion is an eater,
>   A dead lion is a honey jar."

When Samson heard that, he knew his wife had told them. How else could they have guessed? So he said, answering in the style of a riddle,

> "If you hadn't milked my cow,
>   Your lips would not be milky now."

Then in a burst of anger he went into town and killed thirty men. He took their clothes and gave the garments to the Philistines. And he went back home to his mother and father.

Soon, he fell in love with Delilah, another Philistine woman. At the same time the Philistines continued to attack the Israelites. And Samson continued to fight back. In one battle alone, he killed a thousand Philistines. His only weapon was the jawbone of an ass.

The Philistines wanted to see Samson dead. The chiefs went to Delilah and said, "Find out the source of Samson's strength. We will give you eleven hundred pieces of silver."

Delilah said she would do it. She said to Samson, "Tell me, Samson. What makes you so strong?"

Samson made up an answer. "If I am bound with seven fresh cords, I will lose my strength."

Delilah told the Philistines, and they brought her the cords. At night while Samson slept, Delilah bound him. Then she cried, "Samson, wake up! The Philistines have come to kill you." Samson woke up. He stretched. The cords snapped into pieces, as if they were a spider's web.

Each night Delilah asked Samson what made him strong. Each time he gave her a different answer. When Delilah saw that the answer was wrong, she began to cry. "You don't love me, or you wouldn't act that way," she said. "If you loved me, you would tell me." She said the same thing again and again.

Samson couldn't take it any longer and he told her the truth. "I have taken special vows to God. My hair was never cut. That is the secret of my strength — my uncut hair."

Delilah went to the Philistines and said, "Now I

know the truth." They gave her the money and said they would come back later.

That night Samson fell asleep with his head in Delilah's lap. Delilah signaled to the Philistines hiding in the next room. They came in and cut off Samson's hair. Delilah called, "Samson, wake up! The Philistines have come to kill you." When Samson got up, his strength was gone. The Philistines seized him and plucked out his eyes. Their god, Dagan, was in Gaza. They took Samson to Gaza, and held a great victory feast in their temple. Then they said, "Bring in the strong man to entertain us."

A boy led Samson in by the hand. Samson stumbled and fell. The Philistines laughed to see it. Samson said to the boy, "Put me between two pillars, so I can lean on them." The boy did so. Samson stretched out his arms and said, "Please, God, return my strength. Let me pay them back for my two eyes." With all his might he pressed against the pillars. The walls crumbled, the ceiling fell, and everyone inside, including Samson, was crushed to death.

His mother and father then came, took away Samson's body, and buried him.

# RUTH AND NAOMI

famine came to Bethlehem, a city in Canaan. But there was food and work in the neighboring country of Moab. So Elimelech, a man of Bethlehem, said to his wife, Naomi, "Come, let us go to Moab." And they took their two sons and went. Elimelech died in Moab and Naomi was left with her two sons. Both married Moabite women. One married Ruth, and the other married Orpah. Ten years later both sons died and Naomi lost the rest of her family. She had no more kin in Moab.

When she heard that the famine was over in Canaan, she said to Ruth and Orpah, "I am returning to my own land. Go back to your mothers, and God bless you."

Ruth and Orpah loved Naomi. They did not want to leave her.

"No, you must," Naomi said.

Finally Orpah kissed her mother-in-law good-bye and returned home. But Ruth would not go. She said to Naomi, "Please don't make me leave you. I want to be with you always. I want your people to be my people, and your God to be my God. Where you die, that's where I want to be buried."

Naomi gave in to Ruth. She went to Bethlehem and took Ruth with her. The people of Bethlehem welcomed Naomi back. Naomi told them about Ruth. And they said, speaking among themselves, that

Naomi was lucky to have Ruth for a daughter-in-law.

It was the time of the barley harvest when Ruth and Naomi arrived. Farmers were busy in their fields, harvesting their crops. Ruth and Naomi were poor, and had no husbands to work for them. But thanks to the harvest law, they were able to eat. The law said a farmer had to leave the gleanings for the poor. Gleanings were the crops he missed.

Ruth gleaned in the field of Boaz.

Boaz noticed a new face among those gleaning in his field. He said to his servant, "Who is she?"

Boaz's servant answered, "It is Ruth, Naomi's daughter-in-law."

Boaz knew about Ruth. Everyone did. He said to her, "You have come here to live among us. May the God of Israel, under whose wings you take shelter, reward you." He told his servants to treat her well. And they gave her bread dipped in vinegar and parched corn to eat. When Ruth was finished, she beat out her gleanings. And she brought a bushel of barley to Naomi.

Ruth gleaned in Boaz's field through the wheat harvest as well.

One day Naomi said to Ruth, "Boaz is a good man, and rich. He is related to my husband's family. We do not leave young widows alone—that is our custom. The husband's relative marries her. You are a young widow. Wash and dress and go speak to Boaz."

Boaz said to Ruth, "There is a man who is a nearer

relative of your husband. He must be asked first. If he does not do his duty by you, I will marry you."

The next morning Boaz went to see the man. "Will you marry Ruth?" Boaz asked.

The man said, "I cannot support the family I have now." And he took off his shoe and gave it to Boaz. This was the custom. It showed he was walking away from Ruth, and that Boaz was free to marry her.

Boaz married Ruth, and they had a son named Obed. The women of Bethlehem said to Naomi, "God has blessed you. Your daughter-in-law is better to you than seven sons. Obed will provide for you in your old age. He will be great in Israel."

Their words came true. Obed became the father of Jesse. Jesse was David's father. And David became the king of Israel.

# Samuel Becomes a Prophet

Elkanah had two wives, Hanna and Peninna. Each year they went to the tabernacle in Shiloh to offer sacrifices to God. Peninna had children, but Hanna had none. Peninna never let Hanna forget it. She mocked her and made her cry.

Elkanah loved Hanna and didn't care if she had children or not. He said, "Why cry? Am I not better to you than ten sons?"

Hanna's unhappiness would not leave her. She went to the tabernacle. There, speaking softly, she said, "Please, God, take pity on me. If you give me a son, I will dedicate him to you."

Eli, the tabernacle priest, watched her. Then people did not speak to God, they sacrificed. Eli, seeing Hanna moving her lips, thought she was drunk. He said to her, "You have had too much wine."

"I have drunk no wine, my lord," she said. "I spoke to God, asking for a child. If I have a son, I will never cut his hair and will dedicate him to God."

"Go in peace. May God grant your wish," Eli said.

Hanna did have a son whom she named Samuel, which means, "I asked God for him." When Samuel was a little older, she brought him to Eli and said, "This is the child I prayed for. I give him to God."

The people liked Eli's young helper. But they did not like Eli's two sons, Hophni and Phinehas. Both were priests. But they were wicked. They performed

the sacrifice ceremony. People brought them lambs to sacrifice. Sacrifice priests were supposed to offer the best part of the animal to God. But Hophni and Phinehas kept the best part for themselves. Their father Eli knew it, but he did not stop them.

Young Samuel slept in the tabernacle. When Eli was old and nearly blind, he slept there too. One night Samuel heard his name called. He thought Eli was calling and went to the priest. "Here am I," Samuel said.

"I did not call you," Eli said. "Go back to bed." Samuel heard the voice again, and went to Eli. When it happened a third time, Eli said, "It was God calling. If it happens again, say 'God, your servant listens.'"

It did happen again. And Samuel said, "Speak, God, your servant listens."

God told Samuel that Eli and his sons had sinned. "Eli's family will end," God said. "And you will become great."

The next morning Eli said to Samuel, "What did God say? Hide nothing from me." Samuel told Eli and hid nothing. And Eli said, "God is God." Soon everyone knew that God had spoken to Samuel.

The Philistines attacked the Israelites and Eli's two sons were killed in the battle. Eli sat on a chair in the road, waiting to hear the outcome of the battle. When someone came and told him his sons had been killed, he fell backward, broke his neck, and died.

Samuel then became leader of all the Israelites.

# David Slays Goliath

ing Saul was moody and depressed. He looked down and would not speak. His servants said, "Lord King, music heals a troubled spirit. There is a youth in Bethlehem named David. He is handsome and brave. He plays the harp and sings sweetly. Let him come and play for you."

The king sent for David, and David sat at the king's feet, playing his harp and singing. Sweet sounds filled the room. And slowly the king began to feel better.

Now the Philistines again attacked the Israelites. They struck, then took positions on the side of the mountain. Saul sent his soldiers to fight them, and his soldiers were placed on the other side of the mountain. Goliath, a Philistine giant, called across to Saul's men, "Send someone to fight me. If I kill him, you will be our slaves. If he kills me, we will be yours."

Goliath was ten feet tall and covered from head to foot with armor. The sight of him filled the Israelites with dread, and they ran away.

Disheartened, Saul offered a reward. "I will make the one who kills Goliath rich," he said. "And let him marry my daughter."

David came to the king and said, "I will fight Goliath."

"But you are only a young shepherd," Saul said.

"A shepherd must drive away the wild beasts that

attack his flock. I have already killed a lion and a bear—with God's help."

"Go, then, and God be with you," Saul said.

David needed stones for his sling. Taking his shepherd's staff, he went to the brook. He chose five smooth ones from the water's edge and put them in his pouch. Then, armed only with his staff and sling, he went to face Goliath.

"What!" Goliath cried, insulted. "Am I a dog that you come to fight me with a staff? I will feed your flesh to the beasts."

"I am not afraid," David said. "You fight with a sword, spear, and javelin. I fight in the name of God."

David then took a stone from his pouch and placed it in his sling. Although the giant was covered with armor, there was a space above his eyes. David took aim and slung the stone at Goliath's head. The stone found its mark and the giant fell dead.

David ran across the field and took the giant's sword, then cut off Goliath's head.

When the Philistines saw Goliath beheaded, they returned to their homes on the coast.

# KING SAUL AND THE WITCH

avid became a commander in Saul's army. He married Saul's daughter, Michal, and the king's son, Jonathan, became his best friend. David fought the Philistines and won many battles. The people loved him for it. At first the king also loved him, but then he grew jealous, because the people loved David more than they loved him. When David returned from a battle, the women ran out into the streets to welcome him. And as they danced and played their tambourines, they sang, "Saul has slain thousands, and David, ten thousand."

The words cut through Saul like a knife. He sent David out on dangerous missions, hoping that he would be killed. But David escaped each time. Once, in a jealous rage, the king himself tried to kill David. He threw a spear at him. David's wife Michal and her brother Jonathan both warned David to go and hide.

And David and his followers went into hiding.

Soon the Philistines came and attacked Saul. Saul fought back, but he showed no daring. He was frightened and didn't know what to do. In the past he had sought the advice of the Prophet Samuel in times of trouble. But Samuel was dead now.

The situation grew worse and Saul was beside himself with anxiety. Samuel was dead, but Saul had to talk to him. He said to his servants, "Get me a witch who can raise the dead."

"But you banished all witches from the land," they said.

"The witch of En-Dor is still here," someone said. "She is hiding in her cave."

That night the king disguised himself and went to the witch's cave. He said to her, "Raise a departed spirit for me."

The witch recognized him. "You are Saul," she said. "Is this a trap? Have you come to punish me?"

"No," Saul said. "I promise, no harm will come to you. Bring me the spirit of Samuel."

The witch turned, spoke some words, then said, "I see an old man in a robe."

"It is Samuel," Saul said.

"Why have you disturbed my rest?" Samuel said to Saul.

"The Philistines are gaining," Saul said. "I do not know what to do. The spirit of God has left me."

"Then why come to me?" Samuel said. "Besides, your kingdom is over. You and your sons will soon join me. David will be king."

At those words Saul fainted.

The Philistines attacked again just as Samuel had foretold. Saul and his sons were killed. When David heard the news, he tore his clothes and put ashes on his head. "My king is gone! And my beloved friend Jonathan!" he cried. David wept for them. He sang,

*"Saul and Jonathan, how lovely they were.
Swifter than eagles, stronger than lions."*

David then rose up with his men and drove out the Philistines, and the people made him their king. He made Jerusalem his capital and renamed it "City of David." Jerusalem was the most important city in the country, and people came there for everything. But to worship they went to Shiloh because the Holy Ark that held the Ten Commandments was there. David wanted Jerusalem to be the religious center and for people to worship there. So he said to the priests at Shiloh, "Bring the Ark to Jerusalem."

The priests made a great and beautiful parade. In a stately march, and with musician priests playing instruments and choirs singing, they brought the Ark to Jerusalem. David met them at the entrance to the city and marched in with them, leading the parade. In his joy he began to leap and dance, and sing,

> "Throw open the doors,
> God, the king of glory, enters."

His wife, Michal, watched him from her window. She did not like what she saw. When he came home, she said, "A king does not leap and dance for the amusement of the people."

"I danced for God, not for the people," David answered.

# SOLOMON AND THE QUEEN OF SHEBA

avid was an old man when he died, and his son, Solomon, became king. God said to Solomon in a dream, "What do you wish for?"

"For an understanding heart, so I can rule wisely," Solomon said.

"I will grant your wish," God said. "And because you did not ask for riches and honor, I will also give you those."

Solomon built a beautiful temple to God in Jerusalem. Outside, it was all marble and gold. Inside was only the Ark. People came from all over to see the beautiful Temple. They came for another reason as well. They had heard stories about Solomon, about his wisdom and great wealth, and that he wrote poems and could answer any riddle. They had heard he understood trees and flowers and could speak to birds. They came to see if the stories were true.

One of those who came was the queen of Sheba. Her servants and camels carried gifts for the king. She was very impressed with what she saw. The Temple was as beautiful as people had said, and Solomon possessed great wealth. Even the people were well off. They lived in peace with one another. And when she challenged Solomon, and asked him the most difficult riddles she knew, he answered every one.

"Solomon," she said before she left, "the stories they tell about you are pale compared with the truth."

# ISAIAH WARNS THE PEOPLE

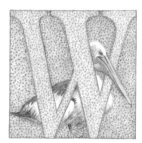

hen Solomon died, the people became divided. One group said that Solomon's son should become king. Another group said no, and other groups had their own ideas. The country grew weak, and foreign kings came in and took over the land. The Israelites themselves became corrupt, growing selfish, dishonest, and greedy. As bad as they were, however, they still made sacrifices to God, still brought their rams, sheep, and doves to the Temple.

Isaiah, the prophet, scolded the Israelites and tried to get them to change their ways. Mornings he could be found on the steps of the Temple. As Israelites arrived leading or carrying their animals to be sacrificed, he cried out:

"God does not want your sacrifices. Your fasts and your feasts have no meaning. God has seen your wickedness and gone away. That is why we have bad kings. That is why the country is in trouble. Give up your wicked ways. Act justly. Open your heart to the oppressed. Protect widows and orphans. If you do, God will love us again. God will come back to us and live among us, as before."

# JONAH AND THE WHALE

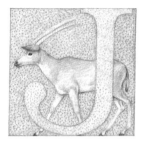

onah lived in Jaffa (or Joppa), a city on the shore of the Mediterranean. One day God said to Jonah, "The Gentiles of Nineveh have sinned. They are greedy and selfish. They cheat and tell lies. Because of their wickedness, I will punish them. Go and tell them I will destroy their city in forty days."

Jonah did not want to go. He knew God, and knew just what would happen. The people of Nineveh would say they were sorry. They would ask God to forgive them. And God would forgive them. So why go to Nineveh? What was the point?

Hoping to hide, Jonah went down to the port. He found a ship leaving for Tarshish and took it. And he went below to the bunks, and fell asleep.

God sent wild winds and a furious storm to whip up the sea. Great and violent waves heaved and tossed the ship about and nearly broke it in two. The sailors were frightened. "Come," the captain said, "let each of us pray to his god for help."

They all prayed, but the storm raged on. Then they saw Jonah, asleep. The captain woke him and said, "Get up and pray to your god. Who are you, anyhow? And who is your god?"

"I am a Hebrew," Jonah said. "My God, the Almighty, made the sea and land and every living thing." Jonah told them he was running away from God, and explained why.

"We did nothing wrong," the captain said. "Look at this wild sea. You are being punished. Why should we drown because of you?"

"You are right," Jonah said. "Throw me into the sea. It will become calm, and you will be able to sail on."

The sailors had nothing against Jonah. They wished they didn't have to take such a drastic step, but they had no choice. They tossed Jonah overboard, and at once the sea became calm.

Jonah was not in the water long. A big fish came swimming by and swallowed him. From the belly of the fish, Jonah prayed to God, saying,

> "God is God on land and sea,
> I was foolish, pity me.
> No more will I run away.
> I will listen, and obey."

The whale then swam to the shore and spat Jonah out.

This time he went straight to Nineveh. And he walked up and down the streets saying, "You are selfish and greedy. You cheat and tell lies. God hates wickedness. To punish you, God will destroy Nineveh in forty days."

The people shook with fright. They fasted and prayed. "We promise to give up our evil ways," they said. "Please forgive us, God." God did forgive them. Nineveh became pretty and busy as ever, and no harm came to the city.

"I knew it," Jonah said to God. "That was why I

didn't want to go. Oh, let me die. I don't want to live."

God said, "Are you right to be so angry?"

"Yes," Jonah said. "They will only sin again."

And he went outside the city and sat down in the road, waiting for it to happen. A hot sun beat down on his head. God put a large leafy plant beside him. Jonah found relief in the shade, and was grateful. But the next day a worm came and ate away at the plant until it withered and died.

"Poor plant," Jonah said. "Poor me, with no shade." A hot wind came from the east, making it even hotter. Miserable and about to faint, Jonah said to God, "Let me die, it is better than this."

God said, "Are you angry about the plant?"

"Yes," Jonah said.

"Did you feel sorry for it when it died?"

"Yes," Jonah said.

"It was only one plant. You did not create it. Yet you felt sorry for it. How must I feel? Nineveh has one hundred and twenty thousand people, and many, many animals. Shouldn't I give those people another chance? Shouldn't I feel sorry for such a city?"

And Jonah finally understood the meaning of compassion and forgiveness.

# Satan and Job

ne day the angels came to report to God on what they had seen on their travels. Satan came from Earth. "Tell me, Satan," God said. "How is Job?"

"He still loves you, still worships you," Satan said. "But why shouldn't he? You've made him the richest man in the East. You have given him wisdom, a loving family, good friends. Take those things away from him and see if he still loves you. He will curse you."

"Let's see if that is so," God said. "Do what you wish, but do not harm him."

Satan went back to Earth. In one day desert bandits stole Job's cattle and killed his servants. Lightning destroyed his sheep. A band of thieves seized his camels and killed his remaining servants. That wasn't all. His sons and daughters were eating dinner together when a great wind came and blew the house down, crushing everyone to death.

"Woe is me!" Job cried when they came to tell him. He tore his robe and wept. Then he said, "God gave, and God has taken away. Blessed be God's name."

Satan returned to heaven. "Well," God said. "You have brought every disaster to Job. But he did not curse me."

"Not yet," Satan said. "You said not to harm him, so I didn't. But let him hurt, let him feel pain, and see what happens then...."

"Do what you have to," God said. "But spare his life."

Satan did his work. Job's body became covered with sores and rashes. He itched and was in great pain. He scratched all the time, and the pain grew worse. His wife, seeing him suffer, said, "Do you still believe in God?"

Job answered, "If I accept the good that God gives, I must also accept the bad."

Three of Job's friends heard what had happened and went to comfort him. When they saw him shrunken and covered with sores, they wept for him. He sat in silence, mourning. So they sat with him and were silent with him. Then Job said, "If I had died when I was born, I would be out of my misery."

The friends, wanting to help, answered carefully. "Have you perhaps done something wrong, to be so punished?"

"I have done no wrong," Job said.

"Are you saying that you are being punished for nothing? That God is unfair?" they said.

"I am innocent," Job said.

The friends continued to ask. "Some secret wrong, perhaps? Something that happened long ago — so long ago that you can't remember?"

They came to comfort Job, but they only made him feel worse.

"I will not argue with you," Job said. "I will argue only with God." And he turned away from them, and said, "God, what have I done wrong? Why am I being punished?"

God replied:

"When I made the world,
And the morning stars sang,
And the angels shouted for joy,
Were you there?

"What keeps the sea in its place?
Do you know?
Can you order the clouds
To bring rain?

"The hawk and the eagle,
Did you make them?
Do you understand how they fly,
How they know where to get food?

"Can you answer, Job?
If you want to argue with me,
You must know the answer.
Then you can argue with me."

Job clasped his hand over his mouth. "Oh, how little I matter. How small I am," he said. "I did not understand."

God then healed Job and blessed him. And Job and his wife had more children and became even richer than before.

Satan had thought he could get Job to curse God, but he did not succeed.

# Daniel Becomes Belteshazzar

I n 586 B.C., Nebuchadnezzar, king of Babylonia, conquered Jerusalem. He took the Israelite king and all the royal families prisoner. Then he removed the sacred gold cups and other treasures from the Temple and destroyed the building itself. He brought the Israelite captives to his capital, Babylon, which is near present-day Baghdad.

Once back in his palace, Nebuchadnezzar said to his regent, "The Israelites are educated. Choose their best youths. Teach them our ways. I will then test them. If they please me, I will make them wise men and reward them."

The regent chose four young men—Daniel, Hananiah, Mishael, and Azariah. He gave them Babylonian names—Belteshazzar, Shadrach, Meshach, and Abed-nego. Tutors came to teach them, and they learned well. But they refused to eat. "Why don't you eat?" the regent said. "I can't bring you before the king looking so scrawny."

Daniel said, "Our food laws do not allow us to eat your food. Give us vegetables, and we will eat."

The regent fed them rice, peas, and beans, and they began to eat. When the king questioned them about history, law, and the stars, he was more than pleased. "You shall join my wise men," he said.

One night the king awoke from a bad dream. "My dream upset me greatly," he said to his wise men.

"But I can't remember it. Tell me the dream, and its meaning."

"O king, live forever," the wise men said. "No one can tell you a dream you have forgotten."

"Then why do I need you wise men?" the king said, and ordered them all killed the next morning.

Worried, Daniel and his friends prayed to their God for help. That night Daniel saw a vision of the king's dream. In the morning he went to the king and said, "O king, live forever. Spare the wise men. My God has shown me your dream in a vision. It is this: You saw a strange figure. The head was made of gold, the chest and arms of silver. It had brass thighs and iron legs. The feet were made of clay. A stone struck the feet, and crumbled to pieces. But the stone that had struck the feet grew larger and larger and became a mighty mountain."

"My very dream," said the king. "And what is the meaning?"

"O great king, the gold head is you," Daniel said. "The silver, brass, and iron are lesser metals, and stand for the lesser kings who will follow you. Each king will weaken your kingdom more, until it disappears. The stone stands for the kingdom of God, the only kingdom that lasts forever."

The king said, "Your God is a great God to show you this." And he made Daniel a ruler in his kingdom.

# In the Fiery Furnace

lacing an enormous gold statue in the main square, the king issued this decree: *"People of Babylonia! Here is a new god for you to worship. When you hear the trumpets, bow down and worship it."*

When the trumpets sounded, everyone bowed down. But Daniel's three friends, Shadrach, Meshach, and Abed-nego, did not. They worshiped only God. The king, hearing this, became furious. "Throw them into the fiery furnace!" he cried.

The three were taken and thrown into the flames.

The next morning, expecting to see ashes, the king looked into the furnace. "I cannot believe my eyes!" he said. "They are walking around in the flames! And the fourth figure is with them—an angel, I think."

The king was too astonished to remain angry. "Shadrach, Meshach, and Abed-nego! Come out!" he called into the furnace. When the three stood before him, he could see no trace of fire on them, no smoke nor heat.

The king said, "Your God is lucky to have worshipers as loyal as you." He then said to his officials, "Let no one speak against the God of Shadrach, Meshach, and Abed-nego. If someone does, cut them into pieces and burn down their houses."

# The Handwriting on the Wall

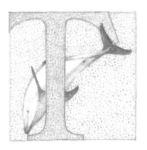

The king died, and Belshazzar, his son, became king. To celebrate, the new king made a great feast. He served his guests wine in the gold cups his father had taken from God's Temple in Jerusalem. They drank and made merry, praising Bel, and their other gods. Suddenly a hand appeared at the wall and wrote: *mene, mene, tekel, parsin.*

"What is this writing?" the king asked, alarmed.

His wise men looked, but could not read the writing. The queen said, "Your father had an Israelite wise man, Daniel. We called him Belteshazzar. Why not send for him?"

The king did so.

"Can you read the writing?" the king asked Daniel.

"O king, live forever," Daniel said. "First, know this. You insulted God. The cups your father took from the Temple in Jerusalem were sacred. Your father did not use them. But you, you served your guests wine in them, and became drunk. You praised your gods — statues that can do nothing. But God who gave you life, you insulted."

Daniel then looked at the wall. "*Mene* means your days are numbered. The same is true of your kingdom. *Tekel* means you are not kingly. *Parsin* means Persians will conquer your kingdom."

The same night, Belshazzar was killed in his bed.

# In the Lion's Den

he new Babylonian king set one hundred and twenty princes to rule his kingdom. Over these he set three regents, with Daniel as chief. The princes were jealous of Daniel. They said to each other, "Who is he that he should rule over us? Let us find a way to turn the king against him."

They could find nothing. Daniel was loyal to the king. So they said to each other. "His religious laws ask him to pray three times a day. In Babylonia, once the king signs a law, no one can cancel it, not even the king. We will catch him with laws."

So they wrote this law: *Show your loyalty to the new king. Rely only on him. Ask no god for anything for thirty days. Ask only the king.* Since the new law needed the king's signature, they took it in to him to sign. The king saw nothing wrong, and signed it.

That afternoon Daniel went to his room for afternoon prayers. He faced the window that looked toward Jerusalem, and began. The princes, waiting outside, threw open the door, seized him, and brought him to the king.

"He asked his god for guidance," they said. "We all heard it. He has gone against the law."

The king loved Daniel, but could do nothing. The law was the law. The guards took Daniel and threw him into the lion's den.

When the king returned to the palace, he learned

of the plot against Daniel. He hurried to the lion's den and looked inside. To his relief he found Daniel all right. "Daniel!" the king called, rejoicing. "I am happy to find you alive. But how does it happen?"

"O great and noble king," Daniel said. "An angel came and stopped up the mouth of the lion."

"Remove him at once!" the king called to his guards. "And throw in the guilty princes and their families instead."

Daniel once more became chief regent. And two great events followed. In the time of an earlier king a writing appeared on the wall saying Persians would conquer Babylonia. The writing came true. Cyrus, king of Persia, the country known today as Iran, conquered Babylonia.

The second event? The Israelites had been separated from their native land for many years. Again and again, their prophets told them they would be back in Jerusalem one day. Cyrus gave the Israelites the Temple treasures Nebuchadnezzar had taken, and sent them back to Jerusalem to rebuild their Temple.